Maths made easy

Preschool
ages 3-5
Shapes and Patterns

Author and Consultant
Su Hurrell

DK

LONDON • NEW YORK • MUNICH • MELBOURNE • DELHI

Draw the shape

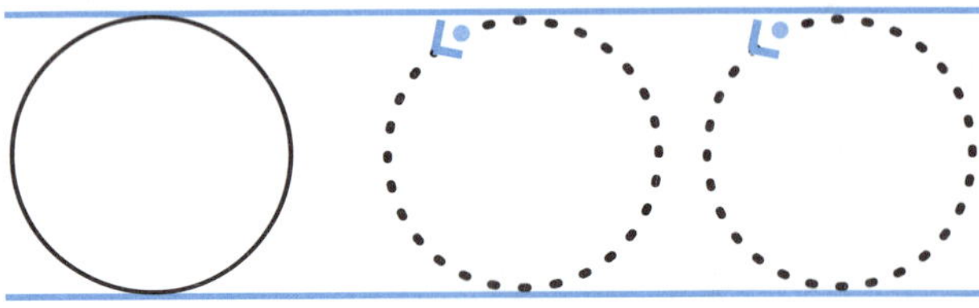

Count how many circles

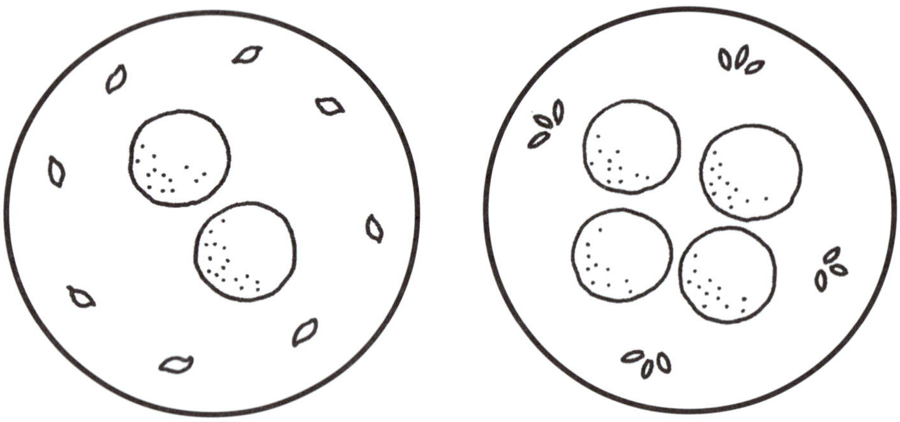

circles

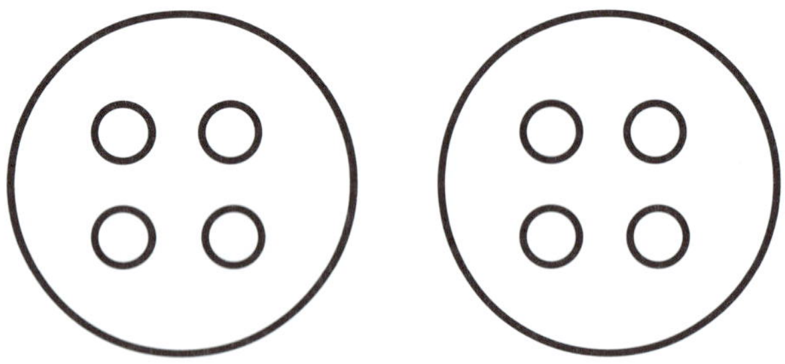

circles

circles

Write the word

blue blue

Colour the circles blue

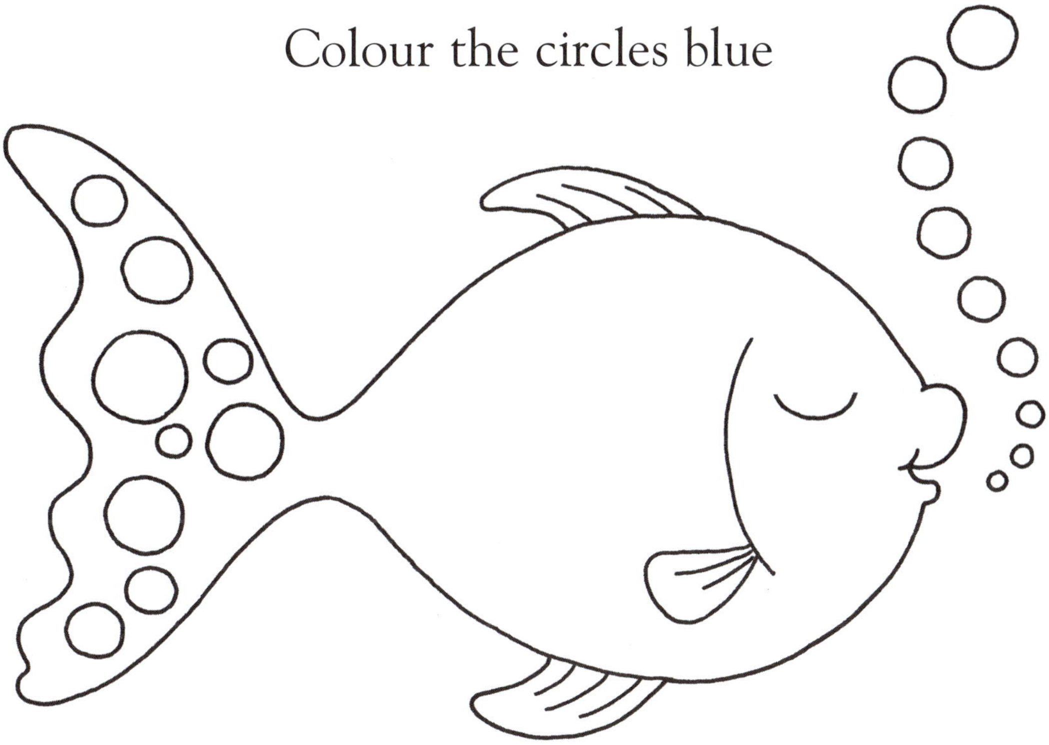

Draw the wheels on the cars

Draw the shape

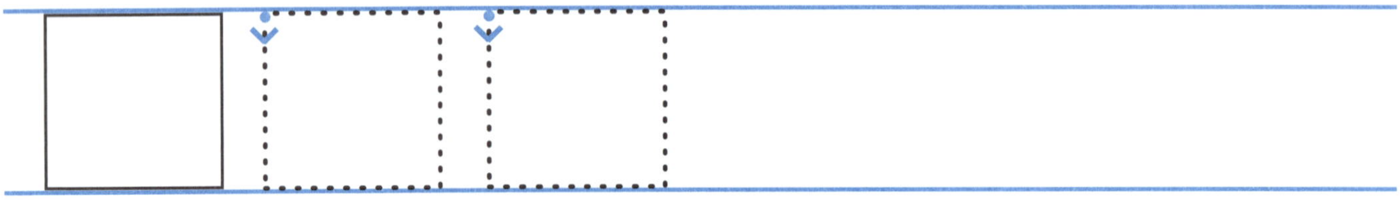

Count how many squares

squares

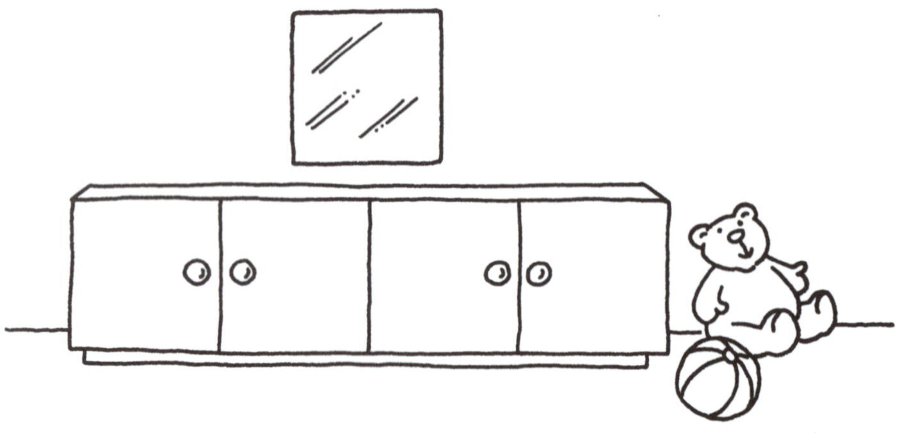

squares

squares

Write the word

green green

Colour the squares green

Draw a square house with a door and 4 square windows

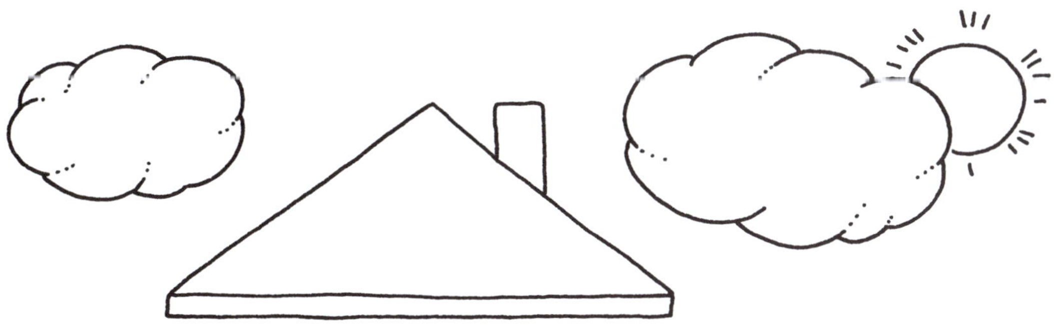

Draw the shape

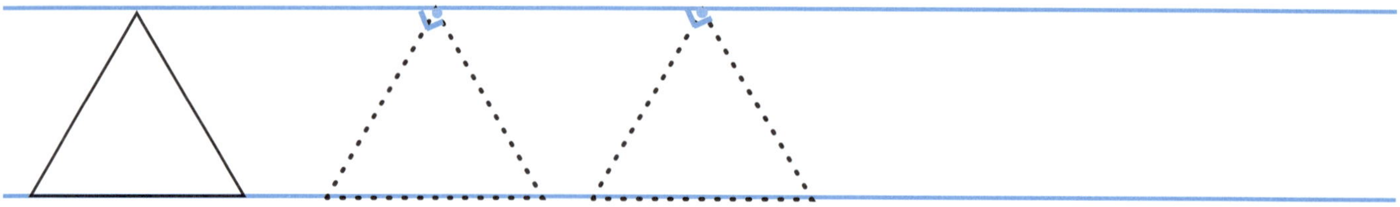

Count how many triangles

triangles

triangles

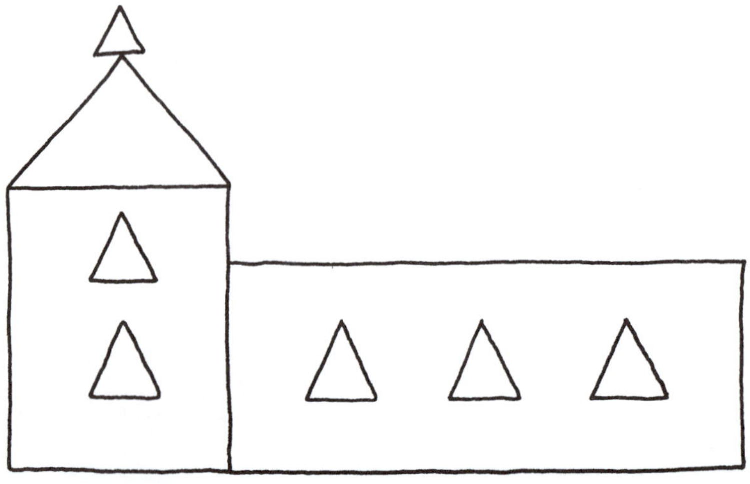

triangles

Write the word

red red

Colour the triangles red

Draw the ears on the cats

Draw the shape

Count how many rectangles

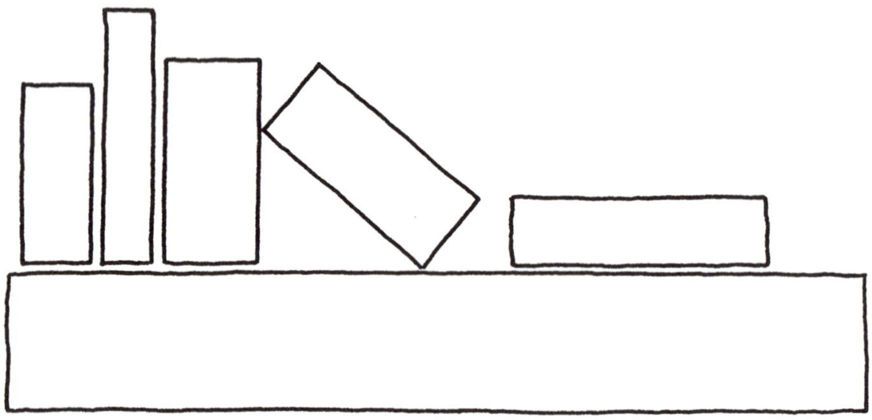

rectangles

rectangles

rectangles

Write the word

yellow yellow

Colour the rectangles yellow

Draw a wall for Humpty using rectangles

Match the shapes

Draw blue lines

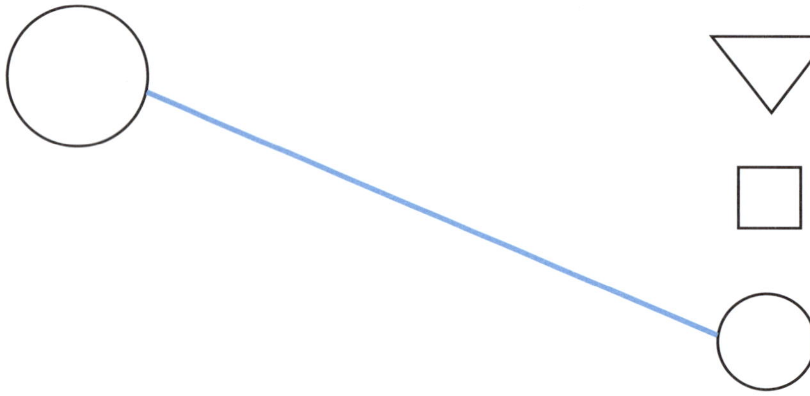

Draw green lines

Draw red lines

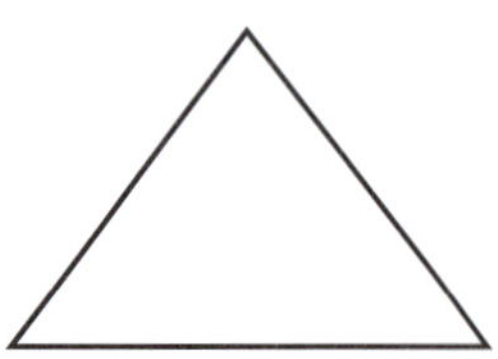

Draw yellow lines

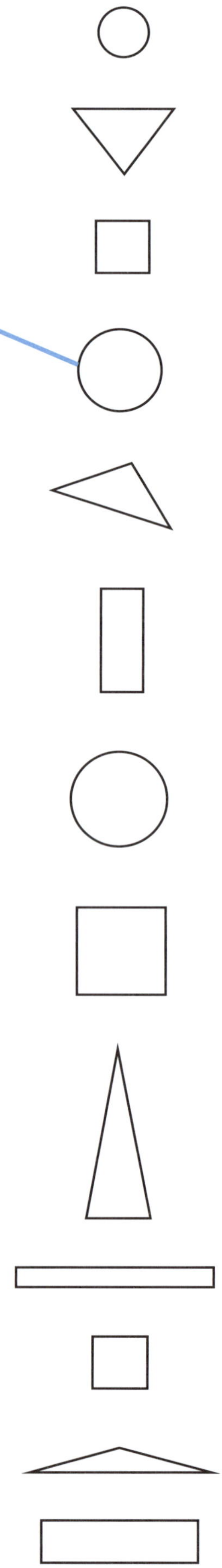

Colour the pattern

circles – blue

triangles – red

squares – green

rectangles – yellow

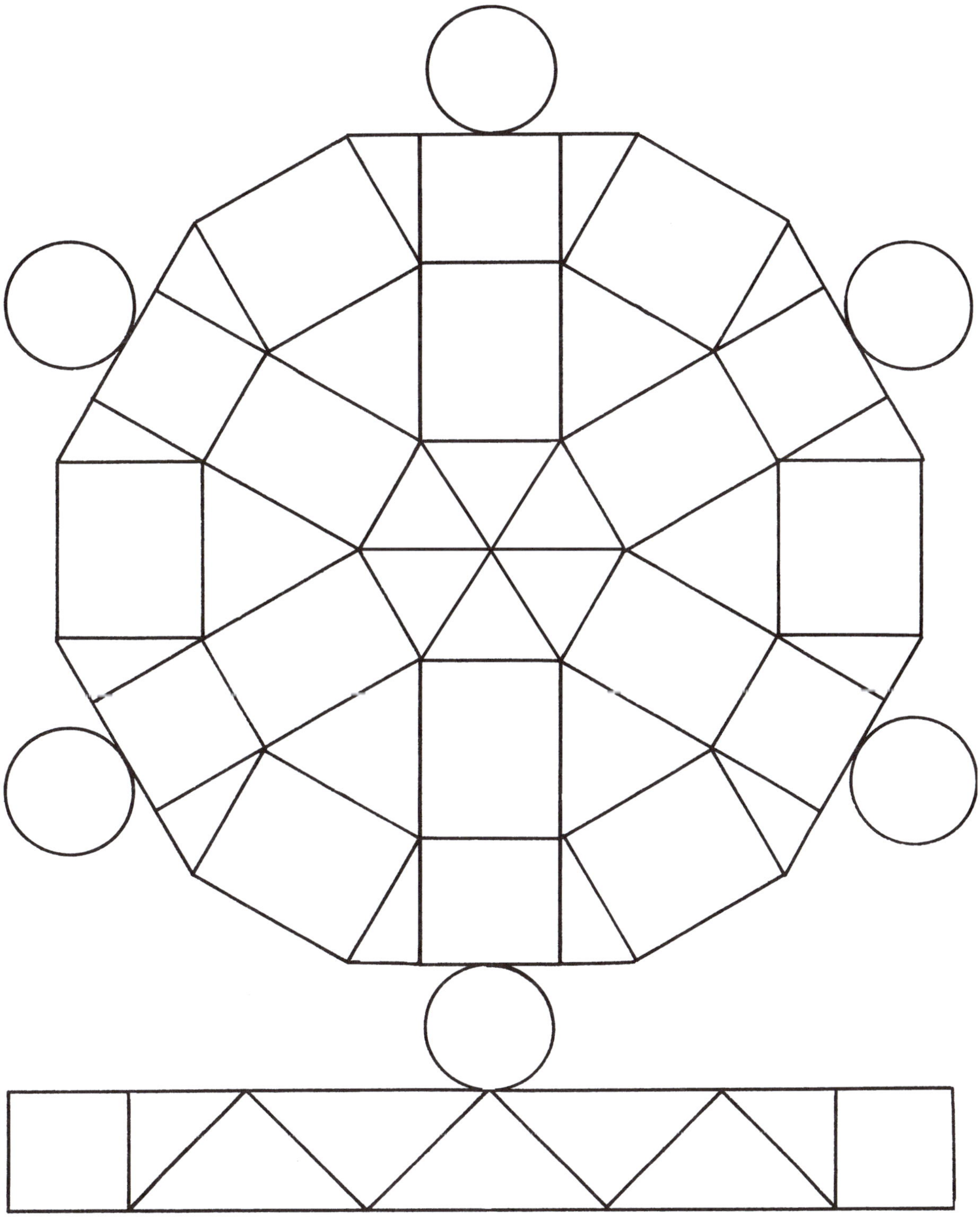

Big, bigger, biggest

A big shell

Draw a bigger shell

A big fish

Draw a bigger fish

Draw a ring round the biggest duck

Draw a ring round the biggest frog

Small, smaller, smallest ☆

A small cake

Draw a smaller cake

A small cup

Draw a smaller cup

✔ the smallest

Long, longer, longest

A long worm

Draw a longer worm

A long necklace

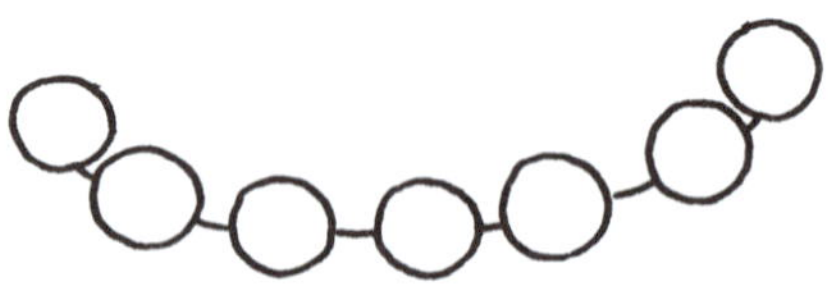

Draw a longer necklace

✔ the longest

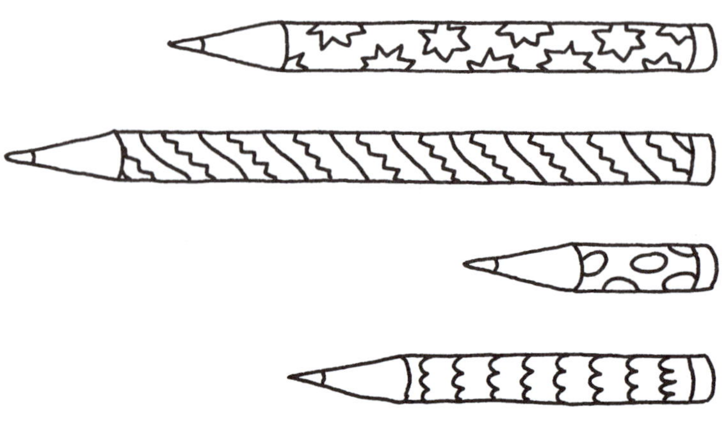

Short, shorter, shortest

A short tail

Draw a shorter tail

A short scarf

Draw a shorter scarf

Draw a ring round the shortest bat

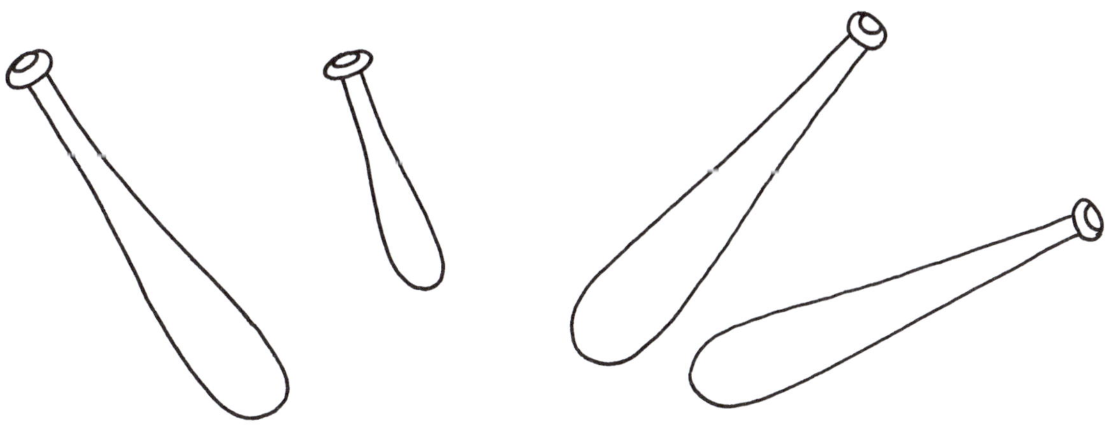

Draw a ring round the shortest worm

Tall, taller, tallest

A tall bottle

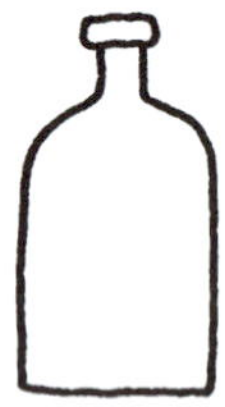

Draw a taller bottle

A tall flower

Draw a taller flower

✔ the tallest

Notes for parents

This book is designed to help your child explore the world of shape, colour, measurement, and positional language.

Content

- Pages 2–11 focus on shape and colour, and include two revision pages;
- Pages 12–21 cover measurement, and include two revision pages for measurement, shape, and colour;
- Pages 22–29 deal with positional language;
- Pages 30–32 revisit the aspects already covered in the book.

How to help your child

A child learns through hands-on experiences, so it is important that your child has had a range of practical experiences before attempting the activities in the book.

This book should be an enjoyable experience for both you and your child, a shared time together. So make sure that your child is alert and not too tired. Keep the time spent relevant to the age of the child and their level of concentration.

Build your child's confidence by praise and encouragement. Celebrate their success.

The pages are designed for your child to colour. This develops pencil control, eye and hand co-ordination and builds up concentration. Make sure there is a range of coloured pencils or felt-tip pens available. Crayons are usually too thick for such activities.

For writing and drawing, your child will need a sharp, soft pencil. If the pencil is too hard they will have difficulty seeing their work and this will lead to frustration.

Talk about the activities on each page and make sure that your child understands what they are to do.

Remember this book is for fun as well as being educational, so stop before your child loses concentration or is restless. This will ensure that the child wants to come back for more!

Page-by-page notes

Introduction to shape and colour

By working through the first part of this book your child will discover the fascinating world of shape and colour.

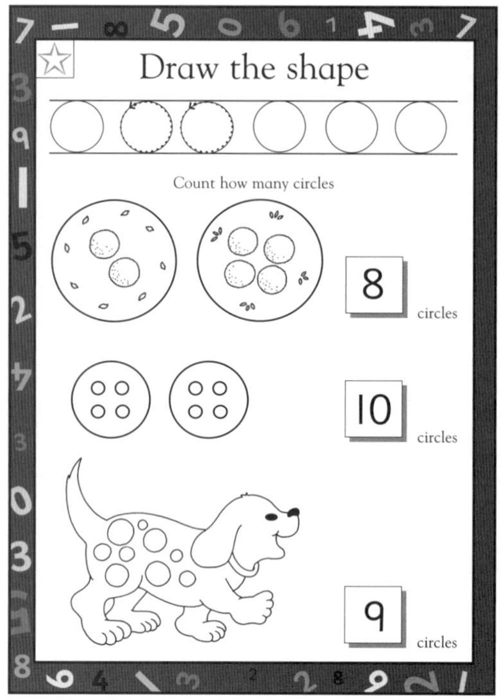

Your child will learn:

- to recognise a circle, a square, a triangle, and a rectangle;
- to identify and match these shapes in a variety of contexts;
- to draw these shapes;
- to recognise colours such as blue, green, red, and yellow;
- to recognise the words for shapes and colours.

How to help your child

For obvious reasons this book focuses on flat or plane shapes, but a young child's first experiences will have been with 3D shapes in the form of bricks, balls, games etc.

The words "square" and "rectangle" are used to introduce four-sided shapes. They are actually quadrilaterals but at this stage it is appropriate to use the more familiar words "square" and "rectangle".

It is not appropriate to introduce angles at this stage. These will be introduced later when your child is at school. However, to help your child keep the lines parallel you could introduce the drawing of a small square in each corner, a bit like a box. This is the sign that denotes a right angle.

Before attempting the pages, have fun with spotting shapes around the house, on journeys, or trips to the shops. Play "I Spy the shape".

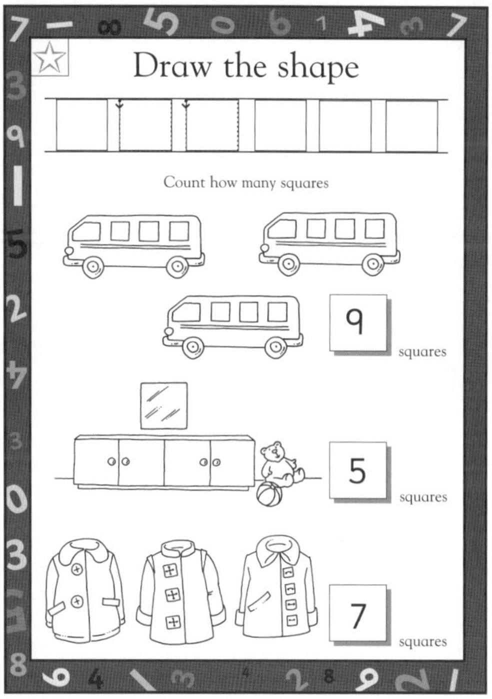

Let your child feel the shapes. How do they feel? Encourage your child to explain the shapes using the appropriate words. Do they have edges, corners, points, sides? How many of these do they have?

Collect things that are circles, squares, and rectangles. Triangles are not so easy to see in the environment as they are very strong shapes and are frequently used within structures as supports.

The four colours that are introduced are blue, green, red, and yellow. Help your child to identify these colours in their environment.

Make collections of things that are the same colour; red shoes, socks, buttons, and bowls etc. To help your child read the word of the colour, make a label and attach it to an object of that colour. Write the word in lower case letters, not capitals.

Your child will probably discover that all greens, for example, are not the same shade or tone. Talk about what they notice. This can lead to many interesting discoveries about the world of colour!

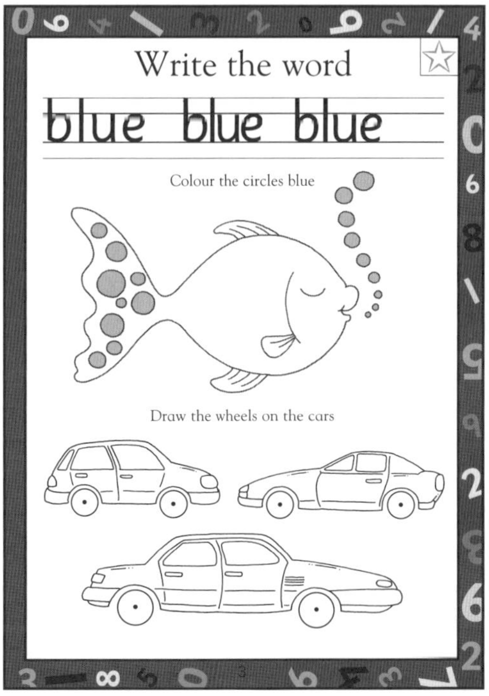

Pages 2, 4, 6, and 8 – Draw the shape

At the top of the first page to introduce a shape, your child is familiarised with the shape and, initially with the help of dots, is encouraged to draw it.

When drawing a circle (or square, triangle, or rectangle) make sure your child draws in an anti-clockwise direction as this will help with the formation of letters.

In the task "Count how many" (circles, squares, triangles, or rectangles), the child has to recognise the shapes and then count the number of these shown. When counting, point to each one individually. If the child is unsure, write the numbers out in a line so they can be copied.

Pages 3, 5, 7, and 9 – Write the word

A colour is introduced and the word is written in dots.

In the task "Colour the circles" (or squares, triangles, or rectangles), your child not only has to identify the shape but also has to select the right colour with which to colour the shape.

"Draw" (wheels on the car, a square house etc.) is the other task in which your child has to draw the correct shape to complete the picture.

Although the text has been kept to a minimum, there are several words which are needed to illustrate the nature of the activities. Read these out loud with your child, making sure they understand what they have to do.

Pages 10–11 – Revision

In the task "Match the shapes", the shape on the left has to be matched with the similar ones on the right. Encourage your child to draw lines to the correct shapes, beginning on the left. This reinforces left to right movement, which is necessary for writing.

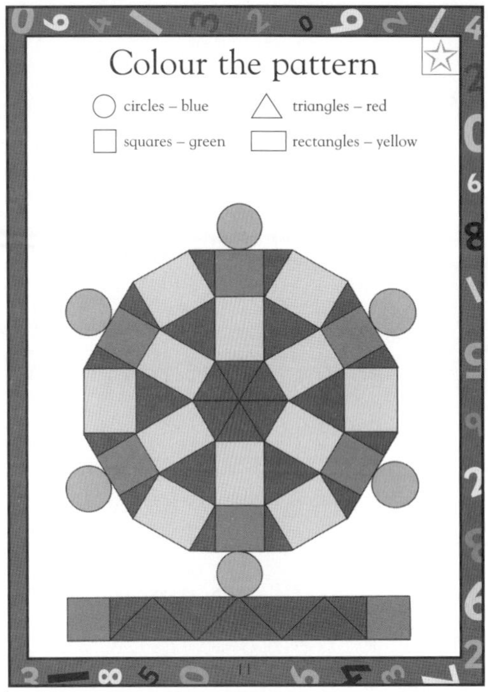

The task "Colour the pattern" reinforces recognition of both shapes and colours in a fun way, by asking the child to colour in a pattern.

After this part of the book has been completed, you and your child can enjoy many activities together creating shapes and colour.

Introduction to measurement

This part of the book introduces the early stages of measuring by exploring comparatives. Your child will learn:

- to estimate the difference in size;
- the relevant vocabulary needed to compare sizes.

How to help your child

Before doing the activities, give your child a range of experiences and introduce the language. For example, collect containers of different sizes, cups, cars etc. and make comparisons between them. Use these words, which are a part of early comparative measuring:

- big, bigger, biggest
- small, smaller, smallest
- long, longer, longest (horizontal measurement in the book)
- taller than/shorter than
- tall, taller, tallest
- short, shorter, shortest
- thick, thicker, thickest
- thin, thinner, thinnest

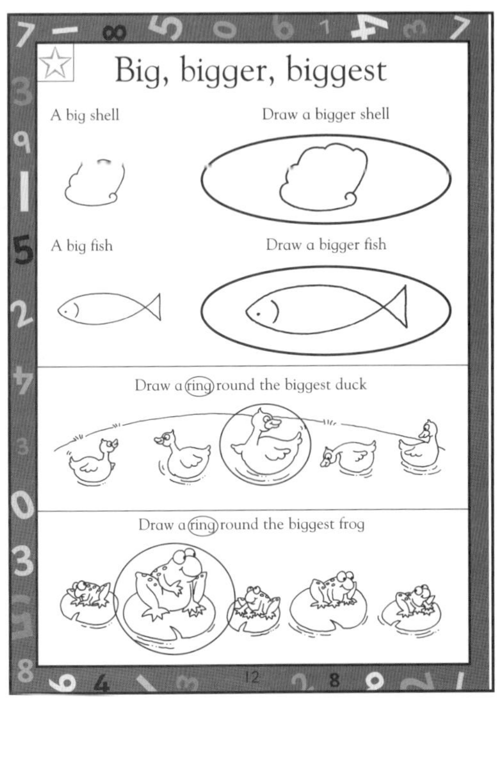

Pages 12–19 – Measurement

The comparatives are introduced at the top of the page. The tasks will include identifying the biggest, smallest etc. by either drawing a ring around the appropriate object or ticking the appropriate box. Your child will also draw a bigger shell or fish, a taller flower or bottle, a thicker candle, a thinner balloon etc.

Each page focuses on one of these attributes at a time.

Pages 20–21 – Revision

These pages include revision exercises on colour, shape, and measurement. Your child may need help with understanding what the task involves, as there are many words on a page.

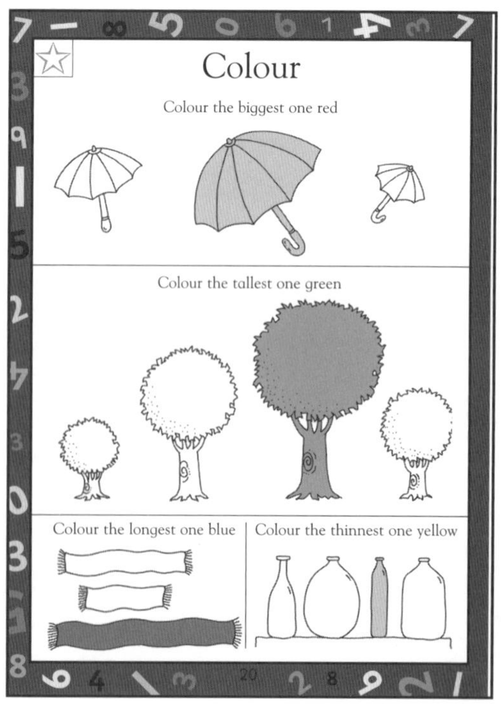

Children need to investigate measuring with a variety of measures, for instance their own hands and feet or your hands and feet, before they are introduced to standard measurements.

After completing these pages your child may become more aware of difference in sizes (and quantities). Encourage this interest and make it fun. Play measuring games. For example, how many cars go along the edge of the table? How many bricks tall is a teddy?

Introduction to positional language

These words are an important part of a child's language and will be used in a variety of contexts at school. Your child will learn:

- the idea of opposites
- words and their positional meaning, including:
  in front/behind;
  inside/outside;
  between/beside;
  above/on/below
  (The word "below" has been used in this book but others like "beneath" or "under" are acceptable in order to establish the concept.)

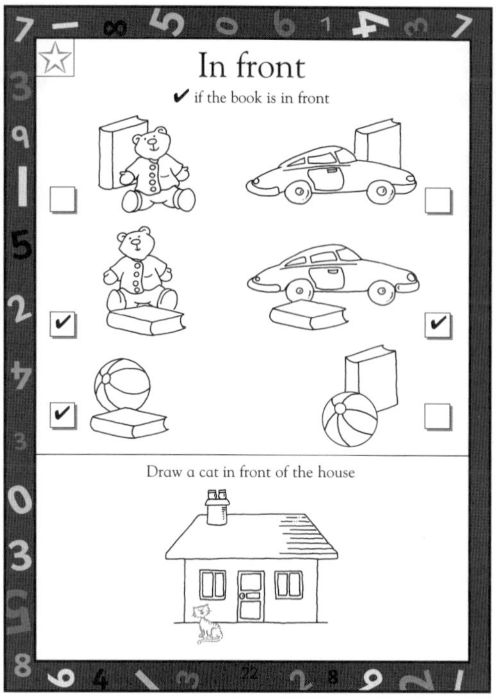

How to help your child

A child gains greater understanding initially by physically acting out these words. So before doing these pages give your child practical experiences.

Play games like "Hunt the..." and encourage your child to give you clues and vice versa. Is the object being hunted beside the chair? Or is it behind the tree? Play "Simon Says". Ask your child to stand on the mat, between the chairs etc. The child carries out these actions only if preceded by "Simon Says".

Pages 22–23 – In front/Behind

These pages feature a book and a mouse. The tasks require your child to tick if the book is in front of something or if the mouse is behind something. Make sure your child is clear about the tasks.

Pages 24–25 – Inside/Outside

Your child has to tick the box if the things are in something, like pennies in a purse, and if things are out, like the magician's hand, which is out of his top hat.
At the bottom of these pages the child has to draw a circle inside a square and sweets outside the jar. This revisits shapes in the context of position and introduces the words "inside" and "outside".

Pages 26–27 – Between/Beside

The first is a drawing page where your child has to draw a ball between toys, and also shapes between other shapes. The last task revisits shape.

On the next page your child has to draw things beside teddy. Your child may need help to read the words. The last task again revisits shape.

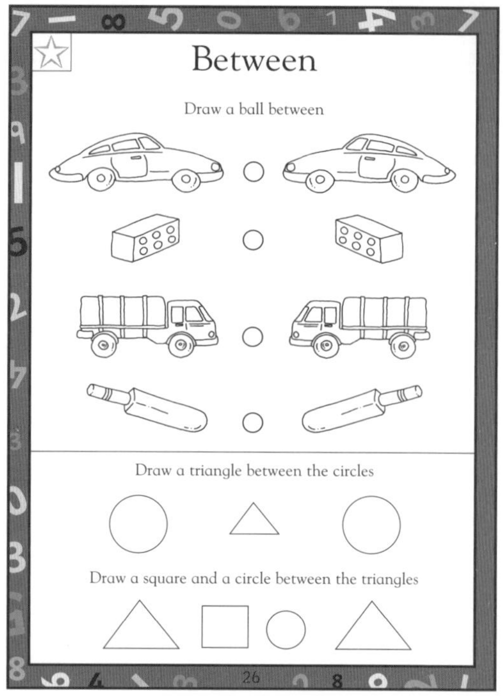

Pages 28–29 – Above, on, and below

These are pages for drawing, counting, and for writing numbers. There are a number of different position words like over, under, below, beneath, underneath, so allow the child to use whichever words they find most appropriate, as long as the meaning and the concept are being developed.

Pages 30–31 – Revision

These pages revise the positions in a fun and creative way. Your child has to finish the pictures of a castle and a fairy. The exercise includes counting and writing numbers, and a lot of reading so make sure your child understands what to do and enjoys doing it!

Page 32 – Revision

A fun dot-to-dot page featuring shapes the child has learnt.

Short, shorter, shortest

A short tree

Draw a shorter tree

A short string

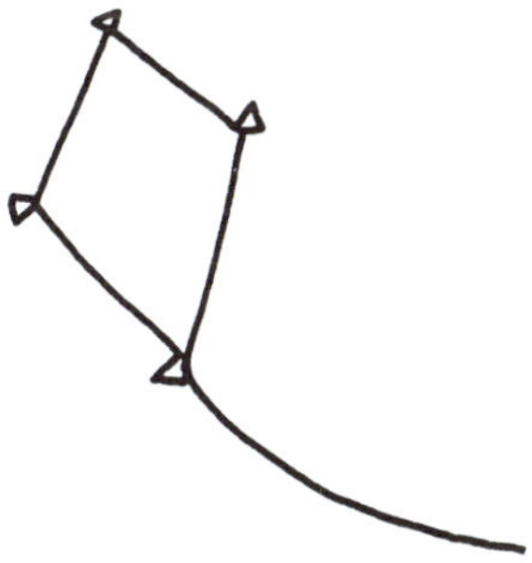

Draw a shorter string

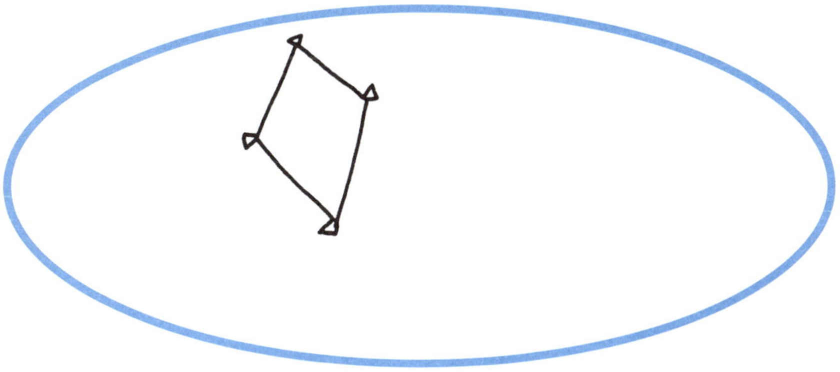

✔ the shortest

Thick, thicker, thickest

A thick tree trunk

Draw a thicker tree trunk

A thick candle

Draw a thicker candle

Draw a ring round the thickest

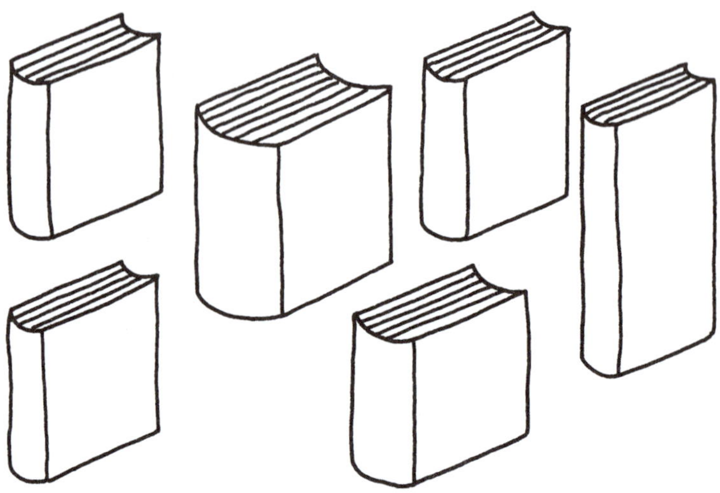

Thin, thinner, thinnest

A thin house

Draw a thinner house

A thin balloon

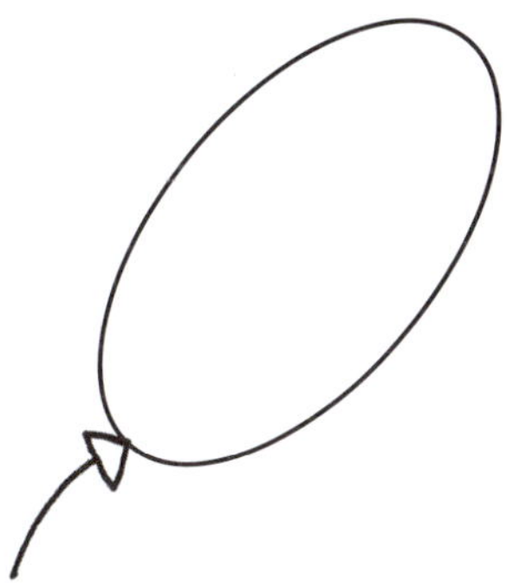

Draw a thinner balloon

Draw a ring round the thinnest

Colour

Colour the biggest one red

Colour the tallest one green

Colour the longest one blue

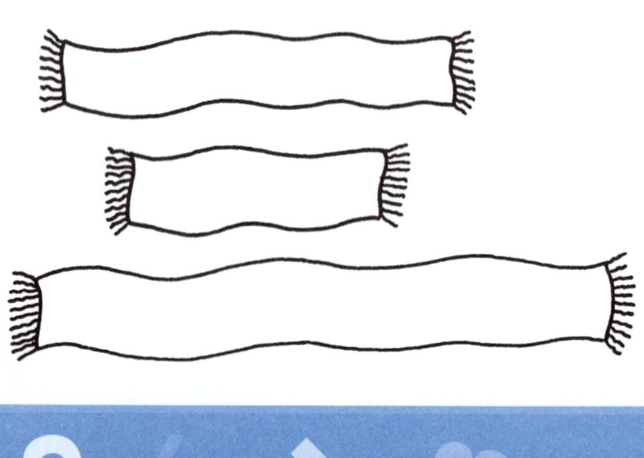

Colour the thinnest one yellow

Draw and colour

Draw a bigger circle — Colour it blue

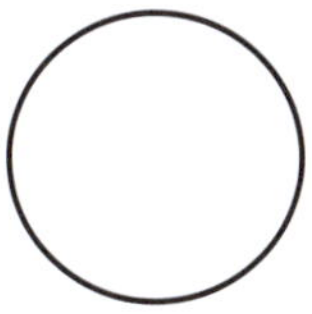

Draw a longer rectangle — Colour it green

Draw a taller triangle — Colour it red

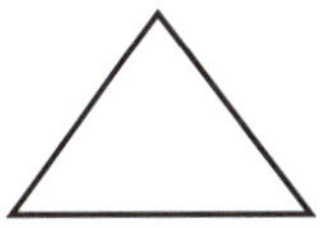

Draw a thicker rectangle — Colour it yellow

Draw a bigger square — Colour it blue

In front

✔ if the book is in front

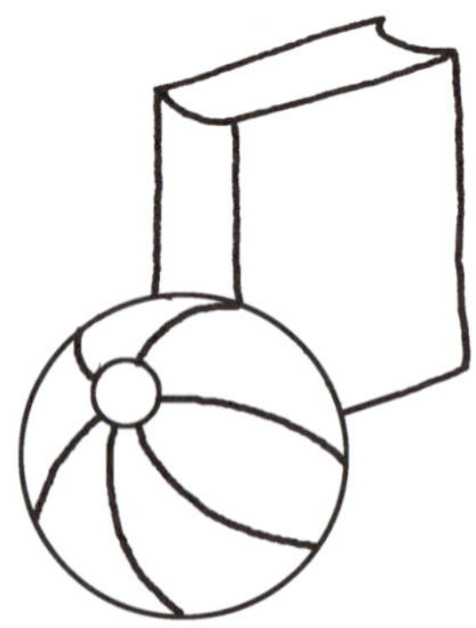

Draw a cat in front of the house

Behind

✔ if the mouse is behind

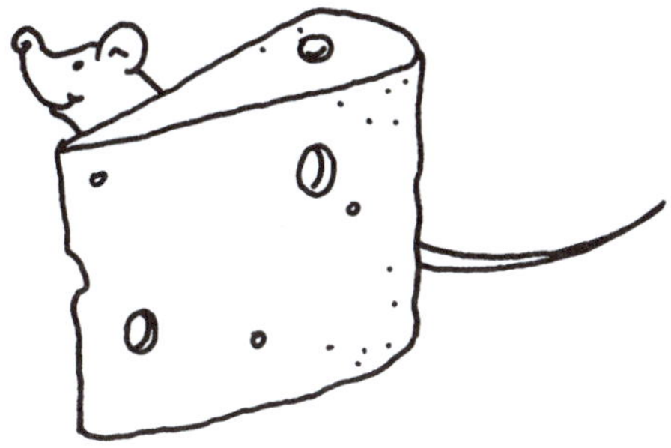

Inside

✔ in

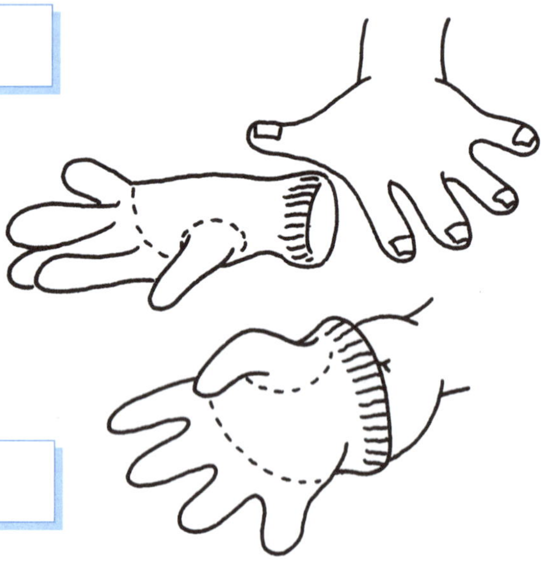

Draw a circle inside the square

Outside

✔ out

Draw 2 sweets outside the jar

Between

Draw a ball between

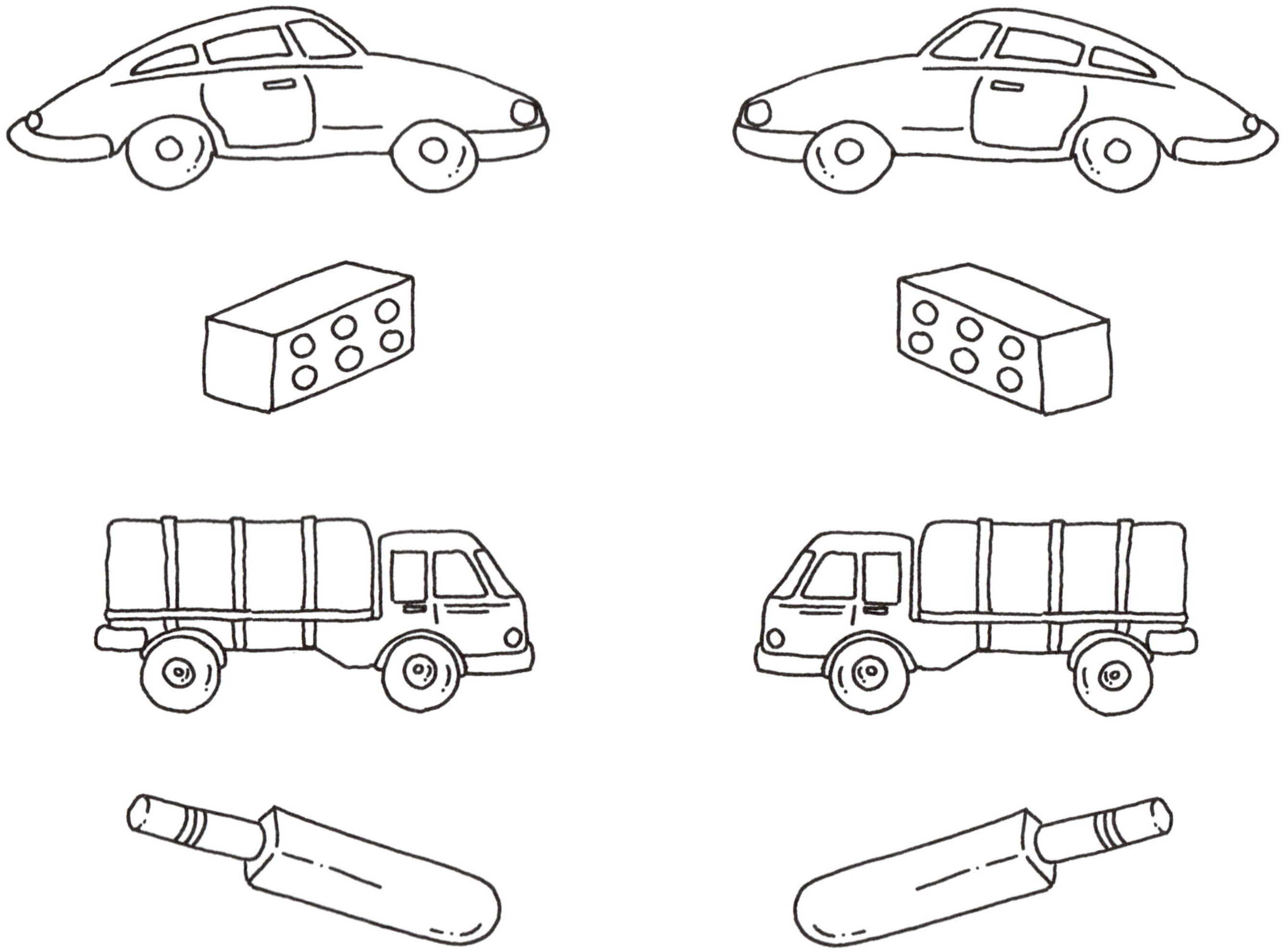

Draw a triangle between the circles

Draw a square and a circle between the triangles

Beside

Draw a ball beside Teddy

Draw a cup beside Teddy

Draw a book beside Teddy

Draw a circle beside the square

Above, on, and below

Draw 2 birds above the boat

Draw 3 fish below the boat

Draw 2 ducks on the water

Above, on, and below

How many things are on the ground?

	on

How many are above the ground?

	above

How many are below the ground?

	below

Finish the picture

Draw a sun above the castle

Draw a door between the square windows

How many circles?

How many squares?

How many rectangles?

How many triangles?

Finish the picture

Draw a frog beside the fairy

Draw a wand in the fairy's hand

Draw some stars above the fairy

Draw some flowers below the fairy

What shapes can you see?